Good Mo
Who's Snoring?

"Good morning, who's snoring?" said Benny.

"Not I," said the sun.

"Good morning, who's snoring?" said Benny.

"Not I," barked the dog, and he jumped out of his kennel.

"Good morning, who's snoring?"
said Benny.

"Not I," baaed the sheep,
and she got to her feet.

"Good morning, who's snoring?" said Benny.

"Not I," grunted the pig, and he began to eat.

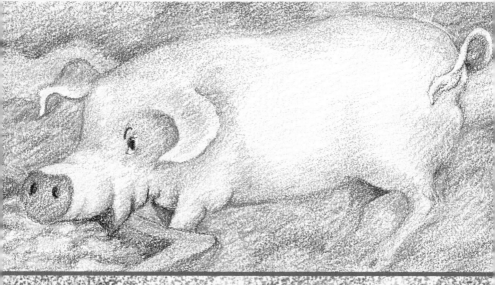

"Good morning, who's snoring?" said Benny.

"Not us," said the hens.

Benny fed the hens.
He put the eggs in his pocket

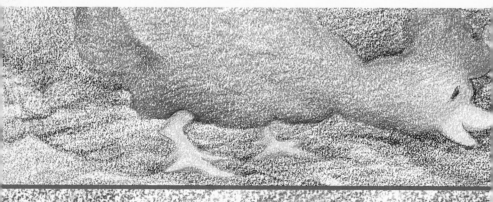

Benny went into the house.
"Good morning, who's snoring?"
said Benny.

"Not I," said Mum,
and she put the eggs
into the pot to cook.

"Good morning, who's snoring?"
shouted Benny,
and he jumped onto the bed.

"I am," said Dad.
"It's Saturday!"